# My Colorful Aquarium

*Aquarium book for kids –
Tips and tricks for young
aquarists*

Denise Melcher

# Table of Content

*Introduction* ............................................................................ 1
*Find the optimal aquarium* ................................................... 3
*It does not work without technology* ..................................... 4
    The filter .......................................................................... 4
    The heating element ........................................................ 4
    Lighting ............................................................................ 6
*The interior of the aquarium* .................................................. 7
    The bottom ground/Substrate ......................................... 7
    Possible decorative elements in the aquarium ............... 8
*Useful accessories for the aquarium* .................................... 10
*It all depends on the water* ................................................... 13
*Plants for the aquarium* ....................................................... 15
*The classic community aquarium* ........................................ 17
*Which fishes fit together?* .................................................... 20
*A brief introduction to the most popular fish species* ......... 23
*It does not necessarily have to be fish* ................................. 30
*The day for moving in has come* ......................................... 33
*Tips for feeding the aquarium inhabitants* ......................... 35
*Important care measures for the tank* ................................ 39
*Diseases in the aquarium* .................................................... 44
*The author* ........................................................................... 46
*Disclaimer* ............................................................................ 48

*My colorful aquarium*

# Introduction

Fishes are extremely fascinating animals because they depend on a very special habitat. Many children want a dog, cat, or rodent so they can stroke and cuddle their pet when they feel like it. You seem to have decided on the interesting hobby of fishkeeping; first of all, I congratulate you on this decision. Perhaps you have seen an exciting report about the underwater world on TV, or maybe someone in your circle of friends owns an aquarium?

are extremely fascinating animals because they depend on a very special habitat. Many children want a dog, cat, or rodent so they can stroke and cuddle their pet when they feel like it. You seem to have decided on the interesting hobby of fishkeeping; first of all, I congratulate you on this decision. Perhaps you have seen an exciting report about the underwater world on TV, or maybe someone in your circle of friends owns an aquarium?

To ensure you are well-prepared, I will explain everything you need to know about setting up and maintaining your aquarium on the following pages. Additionally, I will introduce you to well-suited animals for which you can create a beautiful home. In the beginning, you should let your parents assist you a little bit. Once you have developed a certain routine, you can take care of your aquarium all by yourself. Above all, heed the following tips to provide your animals with a nice environment and to enjoy fishkeeping for a long time.

> ### Tip 1:
> Choose the inhabitants of your tank based on its size and water parameters. Ensure that you don't overcrowd your aquarium with too many animals.

Denise Melcher

### Tip 2:

Allow your aquarium to establish for at least four weeks before introducing any animals. If you use starter bacteria, you can begin stocking a bit earlier.

### Tip 3:

Avoid overfeeding, as it can make the animals more susceptible to disease. Remember, less is more, and consider incorporating a fasting day once a week.

### Tip 4:

Perform a weekly water change of approximately 30%. Additionally, make sure to regularly monitor the water parameters.

### Tip 5:

Always keep an eye on the technology, because after all, the life of your pets largely depends on it.

*My colorful aquarium*

# Find the optimal aquarium

As a budding aquarist, the first thing you need is, of course, a suitable aquarium. When it comes to size, opinions differ quite a bit. Initially, one might think that a smaller tank would be particularly suitable for beginners. However, it has been shown that larger aquariums are much more stable in the long run. Additionally, your animals will have much more space, which benefits their well-being.

Many beginner sets are offered in pet shops, which include the necessary technology. The smallest models have a capacity of 54 liters, which should also be the minimum size for fish.

The so-called Nano-Cubes are usually purchased with a volume of 30 liters. However, the most you can keep in them are dwarf shrimps, snails, or a fighting fish. These nano aquariums are also available in sizes of 10, 12, 15, 25, 30, and 45 liters, but none of them are suitable for fish.

> Remember, an aquarium can never be too big, and many beginners soon regret having started too small.

I would recommend choosing an aquarium with a minimum edge length of 80 centimeters and a capacity of about 110 liters. The larger your aquarium, the more flexibility you'll have in designing it and selecting its inhabitants. Later, you'll also notice that maintenance becomes much easier, and problems occur less frequently once everything settles in. This is primarily due to the larger filters, which clean the water more effectively and prevent excessive contamination, meaning you'll need to change the water less often.

# It does not work without technology

Your new housemate should thrive in an environment that mimics its natural habitat as closely as possible. Unfortunately, replicating their habitat requires the aid of technology, making three accessories essential. If you choose a starter set, it will typically include the filter, heating element, and lighting. These technological components keep your aquarium operational, maintain consistently high water quality, and ensure the health and well-being of its inhabitants, both animals and plants.

## The filter

Consider the filter as the heart of your aquarium, as everything hinges on it. It continuously processes water day and night to keep it clean. Good bacteria break down the animals' waste within the filter, while also controlling algae growth. Aquariums with a volume of up to 120 liters typically come equipped with an internal filter.

Tip: Hide the internal filter behind taller plants.

Larger aquariums require a powerful external filter. Water is drawn into the tank, pumped through the filter located in the base cabinet via hoses, and then returned to the aquarium. With an external filter, you not only have more space in the aquarium but also a neater appearance.

Internal filters should be cleaned approximately once a month, whereas external filters only need cleaning every three months. It's important to

*My colorful aquarium*

disconnect the filter from the power source for only a short time, as beneficial bacteria can die quickly.

## The heating element

Chances are, you've opted for a warm-water aquarium, as most people do. The heating element is responsible for maintaining a constant temperature in your aquarium, which is crucial for the well-being of the animals. While slight temperature fluctuations are tolerable, they can induce stress in the inhabitants.

Info: Two degrees make a big difference for the small creatures in the aquarium!

When the set temperature is reached, the heater switches off and does not start up again until it drops again. The heater, like the filter, must always be powered. Even if it is warmer in the summer, you should not do without a heating element.

The temperature to be set on the heating element always depends on your stock. Most animals feel comfortable at temperatures between 22 and 28 degrees. You should therefore select animals that have approximately the same requirements for the water temperature. Usually, the heating element is attached to a glass wall using suction cups.

## Lighting

You can never operate an aquarium without lighting, because it must replace sunlight. If you have bought a starter set, then this is usually included. Nowadays it is usually LED lighting, which produces cold or warm white light. However, you can also buy special light sources in specialized stores, which make the colors in the tank look particularly intense and vivid.

The tubes are either mounted in the cover or rest on the edges of the tank. If the lighting is too dark, you can always add more tubes. By the way, it is very pleasant for the inhabitants of your aquarium if you can simulate the different times of the day. The sun will slowly rise in the morning and set again in the evening, just like in nature.

As a rule, you should light your aquarium for 10 to 12 hours every day. However, this is primarily important for the plants, because they need light to grow. You will soon find out which lighting time is right because if it is too long, you will have increased algae in the tank.

*My colorful aquarium*

# The interior of the aquarium

Before Before considering the interior design of your aquarium, you must choose a suitable location. Under no circumstances should the tank be placed in front of or near a window. Sunlight entering the aquarium will quickly lead to algae problems. Since your aquarium will be heavy once filled, ensure that the floor can support its weight.

An electrical outlet should be nearby, and access to a water connection should not be too far for water changes. If you prefer less skittish animals, opt for a quieter corner where people won't be constantly walking by.

## The bottom ground/Substrate

Gravel or sand can serve as substrate, chosen according to the needs of the inhabitants. Most people opt for gravel, available in various grain sizes. I recommend a grain size of one to two millimeters. Bottom-dwelling fish, such as armored catfish, prefer a finer substrate to forage for food. In any case, the gravel must be rounded to prevent injuries to your animals.

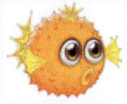

Tip: Use fine gravel with a maximum grain size of two millimeters, because most aquatic inhabitants get along with it so well!

If you want to keep Corydoras, you should at least set up a sandy corner where they can dig to their satisfaction. Filling the aquarium with sand alone is not advisable because plants will not find good footing, and the bottom will become too compacted.

While colored gravel looks beautiful, it's better to abstain from using it. The gravel is often coated with plastic, and you can never be sure if tiny particles will be released into the water.

A layer of four to six centimeters is usually sufficient for plants to root optimally in it.

## Possible decorative elements in the aquarium

Decorative items are not only sought after for their great appearance; they also serve important purposes. They provide hiding places for your animals, enabling them to develop a sense of security. Additionally, they establish natural territorial boundaries, allowing the aquatic inhabitants to divide the individual areas among themselves.

It's important to ensure that the objects are primarily made of natural materials. You'll be on the safe side if you only purchase elements specifically intended for the aquarium.

Info: Roots and stones are also called hardscapes because they are hard in contrast to plants.

*My colorful aquarium*

Roots look particularly great; some catfish even need them to survive. They rasp them off and consume fibers in this manner. In this case, the roots need to be nice and soft; it is best to use mangrove or bog-wood. Roots from the forest or the garden should not be used because you never know if they release toxic substances into the water.

You can find a wide range of different shapes and sizes in pet shops. You can also place perching plants such as mosses, java ferns, or Anubias on the roots. These plants are attached with a thread or using a special adhesive for the aquarium.

### Stones

With stones, you can superbly design your aquarium; there are almost no limits to your imagination. Some aquarists design whole landscapes underwater. You can also build caves or shelters for your animals.

When choosing the stones for your aquarium, you should be a little careful. Some stones can harden the water. If it is already quite hard, this could become a problem. These include all types of rocks that contain lime. You can often recognize them by the fact that they look very rugged. A popular representative is perforated rock, which is often used by beginners. If your water is soft, there is nothing against using them. Otherwise, you can use, for example, lava stones, slate, or dragon stones without any worries.

Trick: Put a few drops of vinegar essence on the stone, if there are bubbles or foaming, then there is lime in it.

## Useful accessories for the aquarium

If you stroll through a pet store, you are guaranteed to discover lots of accessories for aquariums. Perhaps you may find yourself standing helplessly in front of the shelves, unsure of what you need. While there are certainly useful accessories for your aquarium, there are also many things you can safely do without.

In any case, a background should not be missing in the aquarium, as it provides orientation and safety for the aquarium inhabitants. Additionally, animals, plants, and interior decorations are showcased much better. You can either install a structural background directly in the tank or stick a poster to the back of the tank from the outside.

Living creatures that regularly consume food also produce waste; this holds true for fish and other aquatic organisms. To ensure that the substrate is hygienic and free of waste and food residues, you should clean it from time to time with a ***gravel cleaner***. There are models with which you can also carry out a water change.

Normally, water should come out of the tap clean and without harmful residues. However, cities may chlorinate their tap water from time to time without your knowledge. In addition, some copper may also come out of the pipes, which can be hazardous, especially to dwarf shrimps. A ***water conditioner*** eliminates all these substances and makes the water safe for your animals. You simply need to add it to the aquarium after each water change.

It is not only your animals that need food in the aquarium, but the plants as well. They do not find enough nutrients in the water, so you need to feed them with a good fertilizer. It is best to use a ***universal fertilizer*** that contains all substances in sufficient quantities.

*My colorful aquarium*

Sometimes, however, the plants can be a bit neglected. Then you can test them to find out what they are lacking and use a special fertilizer accordingly.

To avoid any risks, you must check the water values at regular intervals. This is particularly important at the beginning to protect the animals from diseases or death. You cannot tell if there is something wrong with the water just by looking at it. Unfortunately, you may only notice that something is wrong when the first creatures have died. A water test is therefore definitely part of the basic equipment. You can check the water values with the help of practical test strips, which check the most important values. Test kits with droplet tests are much more accurate, but they are also much more expensive.

> **Important:** Keep a close eye on the water values when introducing new animals to the tank. Nitrite levels can rise quickly and become life-threatening!

What you need is an aquarium *landing net*; it's best to buy two or three in different sizes. With the help of the landing net, you can add animals to the aquarium or remove them. It can also be used to collect plant debris or floating particles on the water surface.

If your aquarium is well-planted, you usually don't need an *air pump*. However, it can be useful to have a membrane pump on hand. You can use it if the filter fails or if animals need to be moved to a small quarantine tank due to illness. It can also come in handy if you notice that your fish are temporarily lacking oxygen.

For placing plants in the tank, you can use special ***aquarium tweezers***. They can also be used to retrieve items from the aquarium or to feed certain inhabitants directly. You should regularly change the filter floss, which helps to remove coarse dirt from the other filter media.

Regular water changes are best done with a hose that is about 150 centimeters long. To monitor the water temperature, you should install a digital thermometer on the outside. The best way to control the lighting times for your aquarium is with a timer, which you can program according to your needs.

*My colorful aquarium*

# It all depends on the water

Not all water is the same; tap water can have very different qualities. When selecting inhabitants for the aquarium, you should therefore not only consider your personal preferences. What is most important are the water parameters, which you must check in advance.

In nature, animals live in waters with specific levels of water hardness. Some creatures prefer rather hard water, while others can only tolerate soft water. This does not mean that animals will automatically die in unsuitable water. However, their well-being will be significantly impacted, which could possibly also have a negative effect on their life expectancy and reproduction.

Important: Keep only animals with similar water hardness requirements together in one aquarium!

Before deciding which animals should inhabit your tank, it's essential to determine the water values. You can obtain test strips from pet shops that also indicate water hardness. These strips provide readings for both total hardness and carbonate hardness. ***Total hardness*** is measured in grains per gallon (gpg) or parts per million (ppm) and indicates the overall degree of hardness. Different minerals, such as calcium and magnesium, contribute to this hardness.

One of these minerals is bicarbonate, which contributes to the value of carbonate hardness. As long as this is between 3 and 10 gpg (or 51.3 to 171 ppm), everything is fine. *Carbonate hardness* also plays a role in pH stability. You can determine from the pH value whether you are dealing with alkaline or acidic water. This value is also important for the selection of animal inhabitants. The ideal pH value is 7, and significant deviations from this can be very unhealthy for the fish and other tank inhabitants in the long run.

You must keep a close eye on the nitrite values, especially at the beginning. During the decomposition of excrement and food remains, ammonia and ammonium are formed, which can be converted to nitrite. *Nitrite* can be deadly for your animals! If the nitrite level is detectable in the water, a water change must be performed until it has disappeared. Nitrate may be present in the water because your plants need it. Only excessive nitrate levels can promote algae growth.

*My colorful aquarium*

# Plants for the aquarium

Just like your animals, aquarium plants need a lot of care. For this reason, you should choose plants that are relatively easy to care for. There are quite undemanding varieties that do not need anything except some fertilizer. On the other hand, you will find some plants that are more sensitive and require extra light and $CO_2$ in addition to special fertilizers. Therefore, take enough time to study individual plant portraits and compare the specific needs of the plants.

Tip: When browsing online stores for aquarium plants, you can easily see whether the plants are easy to care for or not.

However, also consider your animals when making your selection. Some like dense planting where they can hide or rest. Then there are also some inhabitants who like to eat certain plants. And again, other creatures do not care for plants at all; thus, the flora underwater should be sparse for these fish species.

An aquarium thrives not only from the animals in it but also from attractive planting. In addition, the plants also supply the tank with oxygen, which is why you should plant abundantly. Basically, a distinction should be made between aquarium plants for the front, middle, and background. Logically, plants for the foreground do not grow too high, while background plants can also grow above the water surface.

Furthermore, there are floating plants that float on the surface and perching plants that can be attached to rocks or roots. These include, for example, anubias and various mosses. Finally, there are the ground covers, which you should only use if you do not want to keep animals that burrow in the soil.

In the beginning, you should mainly use fast-growing species because they keep algae growth in check. Slower-growing species can be added after a few weeks. For beginners, we recommend Echinodorus, Anubias, Microsorum, Bacopa, Vallisneria, Cryptocoryne, Bucephalandra, and Hygrophila. To ensure you get plants in the right configuration and quantity, you can order complete sets for a specific tank size online.

Plants with a reddish coloration will certainly catch your eye. This can create great accents and contrasts in the tank. However, you must keep in mind that these plants all need a lot of light and additional $CO_2$ fertilization. Since they are very sensitive, you should wait a little until you have gained more experience.

 Tip: Place the plants after decorating to prevent them from getting damaged.

# The classic community aquarium

Perhaps you fancy a normal community aquarium, where different fish species, and perhaps a few other animals, live. Most beginners opt for this variant. On the one hand, because it is simply the classic par excellence, and on the other hand, they often do not know any alternatives.

In a community aquarium, you will have fishes living together, which do not live together in nature. It is therefore important that you at least choose animals that come from a similar habitat. Aquarists often choose a tank that represents a particular part of the world. So you often see aquariums with fish from South America, Africa, East Asia, Lake Malawi, Lake Tanganyika, Australia, Central America, North America, or Southeast Asia.

Of course, you must not adhere to this; only the requirements of the inhabitants should approximately fit each other, requirements which depend above all on the water values. Also, consider what temperatures they prefer, whether they like a strong or weak current, and how dense the planting should be.

A community tank is particularly strongly oriented to nature, since all inhabitants ideally come from one region. Popular representatives in the community tank are, among others, armored catfish, guppies, neons, mollies, swordtails, danios, tetras, and antenna catfish.

You must ensure that the fish species harmonize with each other and that no aggressive fish can attack the weaker ones. It is also advisable not to socialize too many species, even though you would certainly like to have as wide a range as possible. Among aquarists, you will tend to hear the name "fish soup." You also need to note that fishes often need a certain group size to really feel comfortable. In the end, the aquarium is already sufficiently occupied with a few groups. Of course, there are also some fish that are generally only kept as a pair or individually.

> **Import:** Ideally, only two to three different fish species should be kept in a community aquarium!

Nowadays, a community aquarium doesn't necessarily have to consist of fish alone. Snails, dwarf shrimps, crayfish, or dwarf clawed frogs are often added. However, you must ensure that there are no predatory fish, such as perch, in your tank. In a community tank, there must be enough hiding places and territorial boundaries so that each animal can retreat to rest or avoid stress.

Remember that fish prefer different areas of the aquarium. Some swim mostly at the top, while others stay almost exclusively in the middle, and then there are the typical bottom-dwellers. From each group, you should choose only one or two species for your tank. This way, the fish will naturally avoid each other and won't get in each other's way.

*My colorful aquarium*

 Tip: Start by limiting yourself to one fish species for each of the upper, middle, and lower zones!

If you're thinking about setting up a community aquarium, it's important to ensure it's adequately sized. I recommend a minimum tank size of 110 liters with dimensions of at least 80 centimeters in length. This provides enough space for various species to coexist comfortably and reduces the likelihood of territorial disputes among the fish.

*Denise Melcher*

# Which fishes fit together?

As you've already learned, it's essential to consider the needs of individual animals in a community aquarium. With the vast selection of fishes available, finding optimal combinations may not be easy. The following table should serve as a rough guide to help you navigate this process:

| Fish species | fit together with | rather do not fit together with |
|---|---|---|
| Barbs | Black Mollies, Platys, Characins, Swordtails, Rasbora, Rainbow fishes | Guppies, Killifishes, Labyrinthfish, Dwarf Cichlids, Dwarf Gouramis |
| Black Mollies | barbs, guppies, killifish, labyrinth fish, platys, rasbora, rainbow fish, tetras, swordtails, dwarf gourami | Dwarf cichlids |
| Guppies | Black Mollys, Platys, Rasbora, Rainbow fish, Tetras, Dwarf Gourami | barbs, killifishes, labyrinth fish, dwarf cichlids |
| Labyrinth fish | Black Mollys, Platys, Rasbora, Rainbow fish, Tetras, Swordtails | barbs, guppies, killifishes, dwarf cichlids, dwarf gourami |
| Platys | Barbs, Black Mollies, Guppies, Labyrinth Fish, Rasbora, Rainbow Fish, Tetras, Dwarf Cichlids, Dwarf Gourami | Killifishes |

*My colorful aquarium*

| Fish species | fit together with | rather do not fit together with |
|---|---|---|
| Rasbora | Barbs, Black Mollies, Guppies, Labyrinth Fish, Platys, Rainbow Fish, Tetras, Swordtails, Dwarf Cichlids | Killifishes, Dwarf Gouramis |
| Rainbow fish | barbs, black mollies, guppies, killifishes, labyrinth fish, platys, rasbora, rainbow fish, tetras, swordtails, dwarf cichlids, dwarf gouramis | |
| Tetra | Barbs, Black Mollies, Guppies, Labyrinth Fish, Platys, Rasbora, Rainbow Fish, Tetras, Swordtails, Dwarf Gourami | Killifishes, Dwarf Cichlids |
| Swordtails | Barbs, Black Mollies, Guppies, Labyrinth Fish, Rasbora, Rainbow Fish, Tetras, Swordtails, Dwarf Gourami | Dwarf cichlids |
| Dwarf cichlids | Platys, Rasbora, Rainbow Fish, Dwarf Gouramis | barbs, black mollies, killifishes, labyrinth fish, tetras, swordtails |
| Dwarf gourami | Black Mollys, Guppies, Platys, Rasbora, Rainbowfish, Tetras, Swordtails, Dwarf Cichlids | barbs, killifish, labyrinth fish, rasbora |

> Hint: Corydoras (armored catfish) are so peaceful that you can generally keep them together with all other aquarium animals.

Antennal catfish generally leave other inhabitants alone, but it's advisable to keep only one at a time due to their territorial behavior and strong desire to reproduce. Fighting fish are essentially solitary and are not suitable for community aquariums. Shrimps, on the other hand, usually get along well with most popular aquarium fish, as long as the fish aren't too large.

*My colorful aquarium*

# A brief introduction to the most popular fish species

### The Guppy

When it comes to the most popular aquarium fish, the guppy takes the top spot. This undemanding fish originates from the Caribbean and South America, reaching sizes of up to five centimeters. Since they naturally thrive in schools, it's best to keep them in small groups.

However, be aware that guppies reproduce extremely quickly. To manage this, consider keeping only males or females in the tank. Guppies prefer temperatures between 24 and 27 degrees Celsius and enjoy dense planting, as they love to swim. Therefore, a somewhat larger aquarium is recommended.

### The Neon Tetra

Another frequently seen fish in aquariums is the magnificent Neon Tetra, often referred to simply as Neon. Sporting red and blue bands across its body, this fish beautifully reflects light. Native to the Amazon region, Neon Tetras thrive in groups of at least 10 individuals in a tank of at least 60 liters. They prefer slightly acidic water with temperatures between 20 and 26 degrees Celsius. They can adapt to harder water and higher pH levels.

## The Platy

The Platy, another viviparous fish native to Central America, is quite popular among aquarists. It thrives best when kept in a mixed shoal, typically occupying the middle and upper regions of the aquarium. These ornamental fish come in a variety of colors and are relatively easy to care for, growing up to six centimeters long.

To ensure their well-being, it's recommended to house Platies in a tank of at least 60 liters, furnished with several plants serving as retreat points. They prefer a water temperature ranging from 22 to 28 degrees Celsius and have a diverse diet, including algae along with dry and live foods. However, beginners should be cautious about housing them with swordtails, as crossbreeding may occur.

## The Black Molly

Despite not impressing with colorfulness, the Black Molly remains one of the most popular ornamental fishes. Nowadays, these fish are available in various fin shapes. Originating from Central America, Black Mollies are easy to care for and resilient, preferring warm water with temperatures between 24 and 28 degrees Celsius. Due to their potential to grow up to 10 centimeters long, a somewhat larger tank is advisable. These herbivorous fish thrive best when kept in a shoal and tend to occupy the middle area of the tank, displaying peaceful behavior towards other fishes.

*My colorful aquarium*

## The Cory

If there is one fish that gets along with everyone else without a problem, it is the Corydoras. These cute little fish, which come in many different varieties, can be found in most community tanks. The South American catfish spends its days digging with its barbels underground, searching for food.

They can grow up to eight centimeters in size and should be kept in groups of at least eight individuals. The ideal water temperature for them ranges between 22 and 28 degrees Celsius, although armored catfish can sometimes thrive in harder water. You can house Corydoras in tanks of 60 liters or larger and provide them with dry, frozen, and live food options.

## The Zebrafish

Zebrafish belong to the smaller species in the aquarium hobby. However, since they are quite fond of swimming, the tank must have a volume of at least 100 liters. These pretty, slender fish are native to South Asia and should be kept in schools of at least eight. Zebrafish prefer temperatures of 20 to 26 degrees Celsius and populate the middle zone of the aquarium. Since these fish are quite lively, very quiet species would not be suitable tankmates for them. Please remember to use a cover, as zebrafish are excellent jumpers.

## The Antenna Catfish

This catfish is so common in domestic aquariums that it is often referred to humorously. You can actually keep this peaceful fellow together with all other fishes. However, you should only keep one animal at a time because you will hardly get rid of the masses of offspring. Possibly, two females can go together if the aquarium is big enough.

Antenna catfish are rather solitary and absolutely need mangrove or moor resinous wood roots to scrape off for digestion. As algae eaters, you will often see them hanging on the glass, which is why they are also called glass cleaners or glass suckers. Males can reach a size of up to 15 centimeters; thus, the tank should hold at least 110 liters. The Antenna Catfish prefers a rather dark environment, so dense growth and many hiding places are necessary.

## The Swordtail

This fish earned its name from the impressive sword-like extension of its tail fin, a feature found only in the males of the Central American ornamental fish. As a beginner, it's not advisable to keep swordtails together with platys, as they can crossbreed, resulting in infertile offspring.

Swordtails are incredibly captivating to observe, but they require ample space; tanks smaller than 160 liters are inadequate. These energetic fish can grow up to 10 centimeters long and may even jump out of the tank. The water temperature should ideally range between 22 and 28 degrees Celsius, although swordtails can tolerate slight temperature fluctuations.

*My colorful aquarium*

## The Dwarf Gourami

Dwarf Gouramis grow to a maximum of five centimeters and are usually kept in pairs. These quiet animals immediately catch the eye thanks to their magnificent coloring. Since they are rather shy, they require dense planting in the aquarium. Unfortunately, these fish originating from India are not immune to various parasites and diseases. Therefore, the aquarium should have a minimum edge length of 80 centimeters, with water temperature maintained between 24 and 28 degrees Celsius.

## The Sumatran barb

Among the variety of barbs, the Sumatran barb is certainly one of the best known. This attractive fish originally comes from Southeast Asia and is also known as the four-belt barb. The Sumatran barb has been popular in European aquariums since the 1930s.

Despite growing to a maximum of seven centimeters, these fish require a lot of freedom of movement, which is why the tank must have a volume of 100 liters or more. It's best to keep a group of at least 10 animals. These lively fish prefer temperatures between 22 to 26 degrees Celsius, as well as lush vegetation.

## The Siamese fighting fish

Have you ever been captivated by the vibrant Siamese fighting fish with their extravagant fins at the pet store? The Siamese fighting fish, also known as Betta splendens, is certainly not suitable for a community aquarium. Originating from Asia, these labyrinth fish thrive best in specialized tanks (species aquariums), with males typically requiring solitary confinement.

These fish, reaching up to seven centimeters in length, exhibit high levels of aggression towards others and fiercely defend their territory. Given their territorial nature, larger tanks can induce significant stress as the fish constantly patrol for potential intruders, even when housed alone.

As a result, a tank with a capacity of 30 liters is perfectly adequate for a single Siamese fighting fish. Alternatively, males can be kept with multiple females in a larger tank. These robust fish prefer gentle water currents and temperatures ranging from 24 to 30 degrees Celsius.

## The Dwarf Cichlid

The dwarf cichlid, though not necessarily the typical beginner's fish, enjoys great popularity. Originating from the Amazon region in South America, this ornamental fish fascinates mainly due to its vibrant colors. The butterfly cichlid is commonly found in European aquariums. Dwarf cichlids can reach a size of up to 10 centimeters and feel comfortable even in smaller aquariums, as they are not very fond of swimming.

They are peaceful animals, but during breeding time, they form territories which they then defend. They prefer softer water and temperatures between 20 and 28 degrees Celsius. The dwarf cichlid is quite demanding, requiring dense planting. If your tank is not too big, you can keep at most one male to avoid fights.

*Denise Melcher*

# It does not necessarily have to be fish

When you think of an aquarium, you probably automatically envision lots of colorful fish. While this is still common, more and more aquarists are discovering alternative animals for their tanks. Fishkeeping is an ancient hobby, and many enthusiasts are looking for ways to stand out from the crowd. In this book, I'll introduce you to some interesting alternatives to the traditional fish aquarium.

## Dwarf shrimp

Meanwhile, dwarf shrimp are no longer considered that special, as they have become extremely popular in the past decade. You can keep dwarf shrimp in a species aquarium (a special tank) or add small fish species and snails. Nowadays, you can find shrimp in many fantastic colors at stores. Keeping them is quite easy, and shrimp are very enjoyable to watch due to their behavior.

When choosing, you must note that different species may have varying temperature requirements. Dwarf shrimp grow up to four centimeters in size and can be comfortably kept in a 20-liter nano aquarium. Since these omnivores prefer living in shoals, you should start with 10 to 20 animals.

## Snails

For many aquarists, snails are no longer just annoying co-inhabitants in the aquarium; they can actually be fascinating creatures to observe. In fact, there are some truly beautiful specimens that can provide a lot of enjoyment. Many enthusiasts now keep various snails in a species aquarium, and even a small nano tank of 10 liters is sufficient for them.

Snails are incredibly low-maintenance and undemanding animals; they only require a neutral pH level. If the water becomes too acidic, it can harm the snail shells. You can easily introduce a few shrimps or small, peaceful fish to coexist with the snails.

Popular snail species found in aquariums include racing snails, trumpet snails, apple snails, or rock snails. If there are no leftover food scraps from the fish, you may need to provide additional food for the snails, especially if the algae in the tank isn't sufficient. Some snails reproduce in freshwater by laying eggs, while others like Tylomelania give birth to live babies.

# Crayfish

Crayfish are not yet as common in aquariums as shrimp, but they are clearly on the rise. You can keep them together well with shrimp. Mostly, they are the orange dwarf crayfish, also called CPO for short. Normal crayfish usually grow too big for aquariums. A nano aquarium is also sufficient for the small crayfish species.

With crayfish, you can even do without a heater because they tolerate temperatures between 10 and 25 degrees Celsius. Dwarf crayfish eat vegetable dry food as well as frozen food or fresh vegetables. Avoid putting too many crayfish in one tank, as overcrowding can lead to cannibalism. Crayfish do not prefer bright light; only the plants need light in the crayfish tank. Clay tubes and roots can also serve as hiding places.

# The day for moving in has come

When your aquarium has been acclimated with plants and decorative elements for at least four weeks, you can slowly introduce the animals. It is important not to introduce them all at once. Since there is no stable equilibrium yet, too many excretions at once can cause the nitrite level to dangerously skyrocket. You would not be the first inexperienced aquarist to lose their entire stock.

`Tip: Always add a maximum of five animals to the aquarium per day to prevent a rise in nitrite levels!`

Whether you acquire the animals from a pet shop or order them online, they will inevitably arrive in a bag filled with water at your home. You cannot simply release them into the tank immediately; instead, you must allow them to acclimate slowly to your aquarium. Moreover, it's crucial to prevent the water from the bag from entering your aquarium to avoid introducing any pathogens. Ammonia may have also accumulated in the bag, as the animals breathe more rapidly under stress and produce additional $CO_2$.

Upon arriving home, place the sealed bag on the water surface to allow the fish to adjust to the temperature of the aquarium. To keep the animals calm, consider turning off the lights beforehand. After approximately 15 minutes, carefully open the bag and fold down the edge, akin to rolling up a sleeve. Typically, the bag should float on the surface. To prevent it from tipping over, you can use a clamp to secure it to the edge of the tank.

Next, add a small amount of aquarium water to the bag using a glass or cup, repeating this process every 10 minutes until the volume of water in the bag has doubled or tripled. Then, using a small landing net, gently transfer one animal at a time into your aquarium. Allow another 10 minutes or so to pass before turning the tank lights back on.

# Tips for feeding the aquarium inhabitants

In order to keep your animals healthy and lively, it's essential to provide them with good food on a daily basis. However, it's important to note that many aquarists tend to overfeed their animals. If you've introduced snails through plants, you'll quickly notice their population exploding if you're overfeeding. The abundance of snails is a clear sign of overfeeding, which should be avoided at all costs. Excess food can negatively affect water quality and elevate dangerous nitrite levels.

Typically, aquarium inhabitants are fed once a day, with a fasting day scheduled each week. Feed only as much as the animals can consume within a few minutes. Over time, you'll develop a good sense of how much to feed. Young animals may require slightly more food as they are still growing. If you're going on vacation and won't be available to feed your animals, consider investing in an automatic feeder.

*Tip: Avoid feeding your fish once a week to allow their digestive systems to completely empty!*

# Food types

You can find a wide selection of feeds for your aquarium inhabitants at stores. However, it's important not to simply opt for the cheapest option; prioritize good quality to ensure the health of your pets. Additionally, it's crucial to determine whether your animals are pure vegetarians or omnivores beforehand. Fortunately, there are usually specialized foods available for almost every species, so you can make informed choices.

## Flake food

Flake food is the quintessential choice for many aquarium owners; however, it may not be suitable for all fish species. It's primarily recommended for fish that inhabit the upper areas of the tank. While flakes initially float on the surface, sinking flakes lose a significant portion of their nutrients by the time they reach the bottom. Nevertheless, any leftovers are typically consumed by bottom dwellers. These colorful flakes usually contain a mix of vegetable and animal components, though purely vegetarian options are also available.

## Granulated food

Granules also float partially on the water surface but tend to sink more easily than flakes and dissolve at a slower rate. This type of food is ideal for fish that primarily inhabit the middle zone of the tank, such as barbs or tetras. When purchasing granulated food, it's essential to consider the specific needs of your fish.

## Food tablets

Bottom-dwelling fish, like catfish and loaches, don't typically feed from the upper regions of the tank. Therefore, tablet food is the most suitable option for them. However, the variety of available feeds is extensive, and not every tablet is equally suitable for all fish. These products vary not only in composition but also in hardness and solubility. It's advisable to choose food tablets specifically designed for your fish species to ensure their nutritional needs are met effectively.

> **Hint:** Especially for catfish, you can find special food tablets for each species, so that your animals are supplied with all the important nutrients!

## Frozen food

In larger pet stores or online, you can find various types of frozen food. Common options include mosquito larvae, tubifex worms, daphnia, and Artemia. Just like with any food, different animals have different preferences for frozen options. It's essential to experiment and see which types are best suited for your aquarium inhabitants.

Including frozen food in your feeding routine is important, as relying solely on dry food may not be the healthiest option. To use frozen food, let the cubes thaw briefly in a small glass of water before adding them to the tank. Frozen food is particularly beneficial if you're keeping dwarf clawed frogs.

> **Hint:** From frozen food, you can always create a small stock with two or three different kinds!

## Live food

The most natural food for aquarium inhabitants is live food, but it can be challenging to provide it consistently. Not everyone has a retailer nearby, and live food cannot be stored in the refrigerator indefinitely. Therefore, it's best to offer it as an occasional treat, which all animals will enjoy.

Watching the aquarium inhabitants hunt can also be a fascinating experience for you. Before feeding live food, briefly rinse it in a small sieve with clear water to avoid introducing pollutants or pathogens into the tank. This process also provides exercise for the animals, as they have to work for their food rather than having it handed to them.

## Important care measures for the tank

With an aquarium, you have your personal little ecosystem at home. Numerous biological processes run automatically, forming an ecological cycle. The excrements of the aquarium inhabitants are decomposed by beneficial bacteria, allowing individual components to be utilized by the plants. Therefore, it's important to maintain a balanced bacterial balance. Additionally, a population of snails is also beneficial as they help maintain your aquarium.

Unfortunately, not everything regulates itself, so you'll need to maintain your tank at regular intervals to keep it running smoothly. However, don't worry; the required time is somewhat limited, and besides, maintaining your aquarium is kind of fun.

### Weekly water change

One of the essential maintenance measures for your aquarium is the weekly water change. Not only does this replenish the tank with fresh water, but it also eliminates pollutants from the water. You'll quickly notice that your aquatic friends become much livelier after a water change, and they may even engage in spawning behaviors.

I recommend changing 30 to 50 percent of the water in your tank once a week. Ensure that the fresh water you add is at the same temperature as the tank water. During the summer months, it's okay if the fresh water is slightly cooler to help lower the overall water temperature.

Investing in a specialized kit for water changes is highly recommended as it simplifies and speeds up the process, making it easier for you to maintain a healthy environment for your aquarium inhabitants.

> Tip: Choose a specific day of the week to change the water so you can develop a certain routine!

## Limit the cleaning process to a minimum

There are animals living in your aquarium, but you should not compare them to caged animals. Of course, you need to keep the tank clean, but you shouldn't overdo it. Unfortunately, beginners tend to clean the substrate and the filter thoroughly every month. Often, a gravel cleaner is used to eliminate feces and food remains. In addition, the filter media are thoroughly cleaned with water. You should absolutely refrain from doing this!

> Caution: There are important bacteria in the filter and substrate that you must not destroy while cleaning!

The gravel contains bacteria that break down pollutants in your aquarium. When you clean the sludge, a large part of these bacteria is lost, which can cause an imbalance in your tank. So, only use the gravel cleaner if the gravel or sand is heavily polluted. It's better to introduce a couple of trumpet snails into the aquarium because they rummage through the soil. They are often referred to as the earthworms of the aquarium.

**Be cautious when cleaning the filter!**

It's essential to check the tank's equipment once a week to ensure everything is functioning correctly. This includes the heater, air pump, and, of course, the filter. Beneficial bacteria colonize the filter media, such as sponges. Therefore, only clean the filter when its performance noticeably declines.

Often, simply changing the filter floss periodically is sufficient, as it traps coarse dirt. Cleaning your tank too frequently can reset the biological balance, leading to nitrite spikes, which can be life-threatening for your animals.

> Tip: You should clean the filter only every few months, but not with tap water; instead, use water from the aquarium!!

### Cleaning the glass

It's best to clean the aquarium as infrequently as possible, but you can clean the tank's glass as often as needed. After all, you want an unobstructed view of your little darlings and might want to snap a photo or two. Don't wait too long, or the lime and algae deposits will become difficult to remove.

> **Tip:** It is best to clean the aquarium glass during the weekly water change!

You can simply use a piece of filter floss to clean the panes. Be careful not to get any gravel in between, to avoid scratches on the glass. Alternatively, you can use a magnetic window cleaner, eliminating the need to reach into the water.

### Plant care

How often you need to care for your plants depends, of course, on how quickly they grow and how lush and dense you want their growth to be. In principle, you can let the plants in the background grow until they reach the water surface. You should also trim back plants if they are shading others from light. So, pruning is not only about appearance but also about the well-being of your aquarium plants.

> Tip: During the water change, you can also check the plants and prune them if necessary!

To care for your plants, you will need scissors, tweezers, and a spatula. You can acquire these tools as a set specifically designed for the aquarium. They should be of a certain length to ensure comfortable handling within the tank without disturbing its inhabitants. Additionally, you should use a landing net to collect any plant parts floating in the water. Afterwards, you can fertilize your plants. There are preparations available for daily and weekly fertilization routines.

> Tip: It is better to use a universal fertilizer for weekly application; this way, you won't need to think about it every day!

# Diseases in the aquarium

Even with the best care, your aquarium inhabitants can fall ill. In most cases, diseases result from poor water quality or inadequate hygiene. This underscores the importance of not neglecting regular water changes. By doing so, you can prevent many diseases from occurring in the first place.

However, certain fish species appear to be more susceptible to illness. This may be attributed to overbreeding in many cases. Nevertheless, if your fish are resilient and not prone to stress, they are less likely to become ill quickly. Providing a healthy diet also plays a significant role in supporting their immunity.

The most common diseases include white spot disease, fin rot, fish tuberculosis, and dropsy. These ailments are typically caused by fungi, bacteria, or parasites. It's crucial to recognize the initial signs of illness so that you can take immediate action. Keep a close eye on your aquatic friends, watching for any unusual behavior or abnormalities on their bodies.

> **Tip:** Spend at least 20 minutes each day in front of your aquarium and pay attention to any particular features you notice in your fish!

As the name suggests, white spot disease manifests itself in small white spots, making it easily recognizable. In fish tuberculosis, the fish's abdomen is either sunken or distended. Also, with dropsy, the belly becomes extremely swollen, and later, the animals may "stagger" around the tank. Fin rot is characterized by frayed fins, which may eventually disappear entirely.

If you notice such symptoms, immediately transfer the affected animals to a separate tank because some diseases are highly contagious. If several fish are already ill, you may need to treat the entire stock. You can find appropriate medication at larger pet shops. Normally, they work quickly if the disease is not too advanced.

It's always advisable to keep a few medications for common fish diseases at home. Often, these are preparations that act against different pathogens simultaneously. Usually, a treatment of a few days is sufficient; sometimes, even a single dose is enough. You may need to temporarily turn off the lights in your aquarium as light can negatively affect the effectiveness of the medication during application.

# The author

Denise Melcher has been working in the aquarium department of a large pet store for 20 years. Born in Cologne, Germany, she has developed a great love for fishkeeping through her work. For many years, she has kept several freshwater and one saltwater aquarium in her home. Every day, she advises aquarists on all aspects of the underwater world, as she has acquired an enormous amount of knowledge over the past two decades.

Meanwhile, her two sons are also very enthusiastic about aquariums, so they actively support their mom. The mother of two was able to teach her children about fishkeeping in a playful way because they grew up with it. The author quickly discovered that in this way her offspring were confronted with the subject of responsibility at an early age. Her children quickly realized that an aquarium is not only a beautiful sight, but that there is also a lot of work behind it. However, they also realized that this work with living creatures can be a lot of fun.

At some point, the author felt a great need to pass on these experiences to other children. She gave a lot of thought to how she could convey her wealth of knowledge in an easily understandable manner. This has led to the release of her first book, which should make it easier for children to get started with fishkeeping.

## *Did you enjoy my book?*

In this book, you've delved into a wealth of insights on how to set up and maintain an aquarium, while also learning all about the fascinating world of fish.

Now, I'd like to ask you for a favor. Reviews are incredibly valuable on platforms like Amazon. If you found my book enjoyable, I would be deeply grateful if you could take a moment to leave an honest review.

*Wondering how to share your thoughts?* Simply log in to your Amazon account, head to "my orders," and locate your purchase to leave your rating and feedback.

Thank you for your support and for being a part of this journey.

Yours,

Denise Melcher

# Disclaimer

The content of this book was created after extensive research and in good conscience.

The author does not assume any liability, with reference to the correctness, as well as the topicality, and the completeness of the provided information.

The assertion of claims of any kind is excluded.

*Copyright*

The work, including all the contents contained therein, is protected by copyright.

All rights reserved.

Reprinting or reproduction (even in isolated extracts) in any form (print, photocopy or other method), as well as storage, processing, duplication and distribution using electronic systems of any kind, in whole or in part, is prohibited without the express written permission of the author.

All translation rights reserved.

Sources: vecteezy.com, pixabay.com, pixelio.de, freepik.com

© Denise Melcher 2024

represented by Tobias Schweizer

2nd edition

All rights reserved.

Reprinting, even in excerpts, is prohibited.

The contents of this work may not be reproduced, duplicated or distributed in any form without written permission from/by the author.

We would be pleased to receive any questions, suggestions or feedback:

Mein-buntes-aquarium@gmx.de

Hexentalstr. 2, 79283 Bollschweil, Germany.

Printed in Great Britain
by Amazon